Webs of Light

I0153389

Sakshi Chanana

inner child press, ltd.

Credits

Author

Sakshi Chanana

Foreword

Saugata Bhaduri

Dr. Saugata bhaduri is a professor in center of English Studies, J.N.U , india and has been internationally acclaimed for his erudition and contribution to academic world.

Photo Credits

Cover

Vinod Verma

Vinod Verma, an associate professor of English in University of Delhi, India, is a Delhi based photographer, painter, theatre person and a short film maker.

Author's Pictures

Harish Agawane

Harish Agawane, an engineer by profession and a photographer by heart is Gurgaon based artist.

General Information

Webs of Light

Sakshi Chanana

1st Edition : 2013

Publisher Information

1st Edition : Inner Child Press :
intouch@innerchildpress.com
www.innerchildpress.com

LOC : 1-1056382775

ISBN-13 : 978-0615935591 (Inner Child Press, Ltd.)
ISBN-10 : 0615935591

$ 17.95

Dedication

I dedicate my creative endeavor to the people who shaped and transformed my sentimental ramblings into creative thoughts...to the first and forever love of my life:

My father: Mr. Vinod Chanana- A perennial light of my world.

My Mother: Shashi Chanana- The wind beneath my wings.

My Sister: Shikha Chanana – My first and sweetest experience of friendliness, care and affection.

Foreword

I still remember vividly the first time I met Sakshi Chanana, around eight years back. It was a rather dark wood-panelled office that I was sitting in, and there walked in this young frail girl, her brightness almost immediately lighting up, not the whole of the officious space that I was occupying, but, as a flickering candle would illuminate its immediate surroundings even if it fails to light up capacious vacuous meaningless spaces, a radiant glow clearly spread in the precincts of where she sat.

It would take me several years to realize that the iridescence I saw that day was the radiance of a poet in the making, of embers of poetic thought embedded deep within her, trying to come out and burst forth in this world with an uncanny luminescence. May be, all that the glow wished to tell me that day was what I hear Sakshi cry out today through lines of the current volume: "The incoherence of life / Will make sense / Some day / Till then / Let me live."

Time passed by, and Sakshi proceeded to complete her doctoral research with me, on a topic that she could best consume herself and that flame sitting quietly within her on – "Dreams of Existence and the Alchemy of Love". Needless to say, she researched deep into the topic, producing what would be a first-rate dissertation by any standard.

But, now I realize what her probing soul had really been searching for, all these years ... I hold the result it in my hands ... this slim volume of verses. Verses that wax on life and love in phrases more eloquent than any academic dissertation can ever dream of producing. Lines that flow straight from the core of the radiance I fleetingly saw that first day, on to the pages in black hue, to rebound off them soon, through the reader's ears and eyes, and scatter pell mell in little pellets of light ... a thousand fireflies setting wing in myriad directions.

Now, with these poems in front of me, with the innumerable glow-worms buzzing all around me, their million shards of light reminding me of the original glow that I distinctly saw in that dark room almost a decade back, I think I could have said, borrowing Sakshi's words, which will come to me eight years too late in this volume: "O fleeting moment / Fare thee well / Your destiny / Will defy the past."

I see the promised destiny here, in the pages of this volume. I can but, in pride at being the first witness to these burnt etches the hidden embers have caused on its white pages, the first reader of this volume present the same to the readers, with an invitation to savour the halo that I have been so fortunately privy to.

Dr. Saugata Bhaduri

Professor
Centre of English studies
J.N.U (Jawaharlal Nehru university)
New Delhi, India

$\mathcal{P}$reface

Like the flowing river, that does not give up even in the midst of greatest storms and bellowing winds, each one of us has an invincible reservoir of strength and persistence. This book is an ode to that consistent spirit in you and me, which makes us move ahead, looks over our faltering steps and lets us discover the joy and pain of evolution. It is an accumulation of my journeys within and without: the journey of a child wishing on stars, of an adult trying to come to terms with adulthood, of a woman long lost in the societal maze of norms and her defiance, of a man's indefatigable quest to understand his own drives, of lost dreams and earned hearts, of missed chances and lucky charms, of success stories and failed thoughts, of love and lust, of gratefulness and thoughtful nights, of lost hearts and unbroken threads, of completions and abandonments, of being and becoming...it is about 'you' and 'me'..

Being a poet, I trust that poetry is a sensitive appreciation and observation of the life processes and the continuous transformations that occur in inner and outer worlds. It is a way, a medium to channelize one's unreleased and pent-up emotions in the creative direction. Every poet knows that what makes his/ her poetry readable, are not mere words but the fact that it can resonate with countless hearts across time and space.

This book 'Web of Lights' primarily deals with the twin themes of construing love as an infallible light of the cosmos as well as a kind of web that fixates us to this world of senses and its relationships. The attempt here is to highlight that it is only by immersing oneself into this deep web that one can transcend it and undo its illusion. For a poet, everything is real as long as it is lived on the plane of experience. Most of the poems have been created in different ways of being and thus each of them represents a different aspect of human life: Contradictory and Ambivalent. Such then is the texture of this book... my life...and the cosmos...always changing and evolving.

The idea of this book germinated in an acute desire of a little girl to be heard... a little girl who grew up ...to tell the world that even though it might hurt to love and let go, it is in the empty spaces between these two processes that we become the highest versions of ourselves. It is the I-ness that makes me understand you, we and they.

Through my words, I desire to spread the message of myth of individualism and to allude how all our differences are but a matter of mere illusionary perceptions. My words are intended for the one in despair, the one who has given up, the one who is about to recover his/ her faith and the one, who like me has not bowed before the vagaries of time and nature.

I write to 'become' and to understand my being and perhaps others could also feel some happiness in shared words, spaces and visions. I invite you to share this journey with me...to make me your friend...to walk beside me...and to remember that you are never alone! You are never ever alone!!

Sakshi Chanana

Table of Contents

Poetry

Table of Contents ... *continued*

Table of Contents ... *continued*

Table of Contents ... *continued*

epilogue   87

Sakshi Chanana

Webs
of
Light

Sakshi Chanana

inner child press, ltd.

Being

Life has a way

Of asserting itself

Born out of pain

The first lesson

Acceptance of pain...

The second one

Approval

Dependence

The third

Sensual gratification...the fourth!

Nothing stays

Except the will

The will to be

No wonder then

Being is more important than becoming!

On The Birth Of A Long Lost Stranger

This was the day
You were born
Out of some desire
So I would like to believe.

Though you decimated my world
I created one again
conceived
Three hundred sixty five days
Delivered today- The day
You were born.

In the process
I cut the umbilical cord
That connected me to thee
To facilitate a new birth
To let go of the dead.

On your birth day
I remember you
Like the ones I passed by casually
Or smiled with on a long drive
Better still like those children
That wave from moving vehicles
As I carry on my day to day chores.

This was the day
You were born
To take away a part of me
My star-lit dreams
And your own light.

My long lost stranger
I wish you many re-births
Many re-awakenings
To see anew
A long lost stranger
Who justifies his birth.

Prisms Of Light

In the darkness of night and
Of my soul
I have often looked up to the moon
And wondered
If I could be like it
Shining even with the light not my own!

No, I would rather be a Sun
Shining with my inner brilliance
And lighting the world
Around me
Unconditionally
Even amidst the raven clouds.

I would not be deterred by the rainy days
Or drizzles of pain
Nor would I be taken aback
By attempts of nights
To undo me
Yes, I will be the Sun!

Indifference

When I turn away my eyes
I am
Performing
Either a denial or an aversion
Of the truths I don't want to face
Or realities I don't wish to acknowledge.

When I turn away my eyes
I am
Living
Breathing In and Out
My mediocrities
Or your limited choices.

When I turn away my eyes
I am
Overwhelmed
Motivated by the greener pastures
Or Disgusted by bent in the woods.

When I turn away my eyes
I am
Perhaps bidding goodbye
To what does not serve
My soul's growth
Or your happiness.

When I turn away my eyes
However
Your memories would be retained
In some part of my Iris
And thereon
My world shall be
Realms of lustrous light.

The Masked Woman

If you see her on an ordinary day
You would not even notice
The mask of ordinariness
That she wears.

On some monsoon days
You may find her
Cooing with nightingale
Or dancing with peacock
Wearing the mask of carelessness.

Some hot sultry afternoon
She may be caught
Clad in mask of wind like
Transience
Soothing the weary traveller.

You could be surprised to behold her
Apparalled in the best mask
On rainy days
Spreading the warmth of her love and care
To those gone cold.

You would perhaps one day
Cry in disbelief and astonishment
When you find
The masked woman
Unmasked-

For then she would have
Nothing left to offer to anyone
She would have spent herself
And the masks...

Some Day...

The incoherence
of life
Would make some sense
Some day
Till then
Let me live.

The unwanted thorns
And impossible desired places
Would be visited
Till then
Let me grow.

The relations that withered
And ones that never bloomed
Would speak through tongue of time
Till then
Let me laugh.

The crowning glories of successes
And the steely anguish of failures
Would but be one day, a memory
Till then
Let me create.

The grievances I hold dear
The anger that you wear like a badge
Would submerge in sea of awareness
Till then
Let me love.

The incoherence of life
Would make sense
Some day
Till then
Let me live.

The (Un)Fulfilled Wish

I wished my son to be like you.

Mirror image perhaps
Valor clad
Seeker of knowledge
Personifying innocence untouched by hatred.

I wished...

He could be the master of ceremonies
With your Socratic skills
And possessed your altruistic habits.

I wished...

Him to be touched by same kindness
That you exuded
Unparalleled, invincible
Undeterred by vagaries of time.

The wishes...Somehow
Have withered
Blurred..by my changed vision
I now know
My son would be like "my son".

Farewell !

Fare thee well
O fleeting moment
And when you return
In the synapses of my brain,
Entangled like the unkempt tresses of a beautiful damsel;
I would celebrate your arrival;
Adorn my lips with a smile
Sparkle my eyes with hope.

No...I would not undo your existence,
By painful remembrances or despairing thoughts,
Often was I cruel
To the ones of your kind;
The ones I killed
Still mock at me with helpless cries

O fleeting moment
Fare thee well
Your destiny
Would defy the past.

The Crossroads

As I look deep into my eyes
I see crossroads
The one I have left behind
The other that I have chosen now
I look back and smile
I look ahead and am lost
Directed life...so far
Leaves me vulnerable
To live with uncertain tides of time
How I loved the pretensions of being in control
Feeding the inflated ego and self
Choosing is far less seductive
The dying identity craves for rebirth
The eternal skirmish between who I am and who I want to be
Leaves me baffled
Judgments I would not pass on myself or others....
The crossroads
Do not and would not define me
But the steps I tread!

Streak Of Light

That random ray that beckons you
From the window sill
Has travelled a long way
To tell you about the world of light
My mentor said.

I laughed it off
Amused at his sense of innocence
And concern for me.
What did he know about darkness?
The one who is paragon of light!

It seems like only yesterday
He went away
In search of new disciples
Or maybe his ray of light
Leaving me on my feet.

I think
It is time
I tell him
That my light has travelled a long way
To tell him about the world of light.
Ah! The pain and ecstasy of it!

The Sunshine Cloud

The broken beats of music
And the last empty pack of cigarettes
On attic
Remind me of something
More than rain-drenched moments.

The remnants of endless hangovers
Blank gaze, silent words and
A world to explore in between
The eternity of smiles and crazy tears
Lost in the delirium.

The half-smashed bottles of wine
The hazy vision of love and life
Travels way beyond the myriad stars
Each being-
A universe in itself.

The one in absentia
Cannot judge
The truth about broken bottles and hearts
Or hours of drowning in oblivion
Ay, Captain…we know, where we are sailing to!

The Odd One

Unlike the men I have met
He stands apart
In his subtle and submissive defiance
Of what is right and wrong
To judge him
Would be the solemn error
Of murdering the unborn.

Perhaps his unheard voice
In the long-lost dark jungles of childhood
Makes him oblivious to my cries of concern
Or maybe the severed ties of belongingness
Push him to the lethal edges of being living dead
Each man lives the choices he makes.

Standing at the juncture of here and now
I don't know
What to choose- his maddening race towards Lethe
Or my attempted awareness
That I wish
Could seep deep down
Into his heart and soul.

My gifts of awareness and responsibility
Bind me to him
As would be a drop of water
To the last end of shallow stretch of river
Can I choose for him;
What he himself does not!
Much like other men I have met, I cannot!

Being Single

Your long deep silences
And the solitary world of your gaze
Reminds me of the old superstition
Of spotting two crows as a good omen
And one as harbinger of sorrow.

Growing up
With idioms and phrases
Of plurality as power
In nature as well as life
Pondering over life's designs
Is it that when singularity fails
Plurality is born
Or is it the immense strength of one
That scares us away and thus divides us
In the name of caste, color and creed?

As if that did not suffice
I fit in so well in the plural roles
Of beloved, sister, daughter and friend
As does my counterpart
As father, brother, son and companion
I intend to undo this sinister design
Of those higher beings
To mock at the silence of a bird of awareness
Who just happens to perch upon
Their branched alleys of conscience.

Now, The black-eyed crow
The Raven and the eagle
Stand not for loneliness
But the strength of aloneness
Yes..Awareness is all!

Walls

I build walls,
Walls that protect,
Walls that shield,
Walls that say- I shall not yield
Or reveal
Who I am or How I feel.

I build walls,
Walls that hide,
Walls that smother what is inside,
Walls that stare or smile
or look away,
Silent lies .

Walls that block even my own eyes
For meeting with the tears I might have cried
I build walls,
Walls that never let me truly touch
The ones I love so much

Walls that need to fall,
Walls meant to be fortress
Are prisons after all!

A Woman in Future..

This Instant
I am a woman in future
Looking back at my past
The first love
The beginnings of an endless journey
Into the ocean of otherness.

Intelligence came along the desire to learn
Or probably prove
Sweetness and kindness acquired
Oars to sail through
The tumultuous waters of existence
And chaotic sea of emotions.

It is all a patterned maze
The ones with lost childhood
Fitted in my child-like utopian ideals
Those colored by joys of extravagant living
Found solemn seriousness in my thoughtful musings
Blending with me like the dew on the early morning rose.

Some appealed to personal ideals of perfection
Euphoric meetings
An acute sense of being understood
Camouflaged beings
Lost in self or mutual admiration
Till sameness induced a secret repulsion.

There were others, innocence personified
Or worn as a mask
To defer responsibility
May be the deep pain of lovelessness
I tended to their glass-like worlds
Incredibly believing in their transparency and truth.

Some were muddled beings
Looking up to me, in certain deified manner
Glorifying and acknowledging my less hazy pictures
Compared to their discolored and disfigured mental images
For me, they gave up what they could
Self-sacrifice has its own charms.

A couple of them
Made visible
The beauty of balance
Giving and Receiving
Freedom and togetherness
Grateful I am, to them.

This instant
I am a woman in future
Looking back at my past
And I know
It has been an amazing journey
The tiny steps of time have created
Endless Ripples of bliss and peace.

Desire

Desire, a capricious woman
Attends only to its own flights
Of imagination and creativity
The poor beau, reason..Sighs.

I desire you like an adventure
An experiment, an uncharted territory
A thrill…
Where I can meet the unknown 'me'.

Your desire for me
Is that pristine yearning
For the mirror image
Where you can feel at home.

I could stay with you like a memory
Of a rose, dried up in a book
Or like a reality
Draping you in the fragrance of love.

The winds of time
Either sustain or annihilate desire
It won't matter much though
Having stolen some kisses and glances.

My desires have wings and know
That somewhere I am awaited:
The dim-lit streets, the rain-fed earth
The soiled pages in some long forgotten book-stack.

Your footsteps might halt and move
In search of your lost longings
Or the remembrance of things past
Which neither hurt nor heal.

Stay close, if you dare
Risk the uncertainty of feelings
The transience of life
The complete oblivion.

The ecstasies of merger or union
Are worth when we let each other fly
On the wings of desire
What a bliss home-coming!

Let It Be

Much have I traveled in the realms of love and betrayal
The terrains of happiness and gratitude
The wayward ways of heart and mind
Standing at the threshold of today
New roads, new people, new beginnings
Await.

I am in no haste though
To pin any relation with a name tag
Or to drape it with past pains or future hopes
The uniqueness of this moment
Appeasing and inviting
Assures unprecedented peace and bliss.

O wonderful life
Your seduction is final
And I would just sing along
Like a bird who is aware
That if he chooses, the whole sky is home
That love he seeks is nearer than he thought.

I would not be Icarus
My waxen wings
Know that the fiery passion of the sun is not my ally
That the winds of change are inevitable
For they are the pathways to my soul's calling
I would see and reach, where I must
And not necessarily where I desire
Yes, I would not be Icarus.

Ember

Now I miss you,
More like a moment
That shall come to life
Again
In the time-space shift
Facilitated with a leap of faith.

The last ember glowing
Seduces the fire
To stay in close proximity
With the Earth
Not to die
Of arrogance

The earthiness of me
Is a match to your flickering fieriness
Only if you were not so adamant
To burn the hands that
Reach to caress and cajole
The ember would sustain the fire.

Exile

Today, I disown you
From the precincts of my heart and soul
It is not because I hate you
Or have reservoirs of unleashed anger
Neither am I perturbed by your apathy
Nor by my long, consistent hurts.

It is just the awareness of dis-connect
That I feel in the depth of your eyes
And the new-found freedom of my being
Now you don't matter the way you did
Now I matter more
To myself.

You have nothing left to offer me
A doting look, an empathetic concern or an
acknowledgment
Not that I need them
But your cup is full
You are incapable of giving now
For the desire is long dead.

Today, I disown you
Ironically, it is only the river
That can quench the thirst
And not the sea
Your big-ness does not serve me well
I would be a river unto myself.

Nothingness

When you take away from me
What makes me "me"
I am left with an empty feeling
In my heart

This is what it must be like
To lie in mother's womb
Or to experience
Epiphany

Child-like, I am
In the moment
Thousand things to enchant me
And I don't know where to begin.

The world is my playground
I pick and choose
What enthralls
Not hating what does not.

The stale –identity

Creeps in, clandestinely

To mock at new-found freedom

The skirmish has begun.

This time, it has to give way

To what I was born to be

The created realm of being

Shall undo..the inherited scheme of things.

In the battleground of 'now'

I shall play the games of my choice

And not the ones

I must.

Yes, the chaos must precede

The organization

And organization must lead to chaos

Till no-thing is left…facilitating creation.

Will To Be...

My words seem to die
A slow painful death
With an attempted murder
Of our love
Or Shall I say habit?

Wishfully,
Skillfully,
Smothering any way
That connects us
Wonder if any ember can kindle it again?

Death separates everyone eventually
Why do we create the spaces of non-existence;
For the people
When they are alive!

My chiseled inanimate existence, carefully crafted by you
Hurts, but does not deter me
Nay,
I won't let you die
Before your time.

You shall come to life
In every moment
A tear trickles down
My soul
You shall breathe
With the random ramblings of my mind.

My lost-present love
You would walk oblivious
In the terrains of my heart
Tired,
When you would sleep
I shall enclose you in my arms.

You must outlive
What you have created
And who you have become
My love- you shall be more than a speck in the universe
For my words, though dying shall immortalize you!

The Man Who Sold Happiness

In one corner of the life-street
A man sells happiness
I ordered some
Even paid him through a debit card.

But it has been ages
Since I received the parcel
I believe he must be busy with other clients
The richer ones, the luckier ones.

Or maybe he is just running out of stock
Expensive and rare as it is
Perhaps there have been some serious
Problems in his professional and personal life.

Wait! I have got a Parcel
Eureka! It must be happiness!
What? How is it possible?
It is just a mirror…

Duly signed by the shop-owner

Carrying a post-card,

Tucked with it

A 'sorry for delay and inconvenience' note.

On the handle of mirror are engraved

Tiny golden words

Your parcel of happiness

Is reflected in the mirror.

Some lessons come too late

Walking in the life-street

I therefore choose from here-on

Never to buy or sell.

But to be

A creator

Creating happiness.

Walk A Little

You say, ' I am tired of the endless journeys and its
deviations; And
the paths that seem to obscure the very vision that helped to
create them;
The boulders of disappointments weigh heavy on my soul,
The heart is sore with smithereens of pebbles pointing
inwards,
The faltering steps...hate to dwindle
The dimmed vision...searches for the lost sparkle
The gifts of faith and confidence seem to wither away
The wait is perhaps, not worth it...'.

They say, ' Things come easy, the journey is not needed
We are the ones born with a silver spoon
Disappointments have not been our lot
And we do not wonder about the here-after questions
The heart is just in in its place...doing what it should
Pumping the blood
There is plenty to be wasted and again,
The wait for anything, perhaps, is not worth it...

He says, ' The journey is fun and adventure, thrilling

The fear-filled moments emanate courage

Flight or fright...the choice is mine

Cowering in mire of self-pity

Is not a warrior's lineament

Strive, Strike...Stay

The wait, perhaps, is sometimes, worth it...

I say, ' The journey in itself is a process

The faltering steps, the disappointed soul;

The sore heart and the dimmed vision

The defeated hands, the teary eyes

The coveted success and the dreaded sadness

The distant goals and weary determination

Walk a little, my dear friend;

The wait, perhaps, is always worth it...

Gifts

You can take away your gifts from me,

I won't stop you

The innocence intimidated by corrupt experiences,

The presence of your absence

The absence of your presence

Love aborted by rationality

Kindness compromised for greater anticipated gains

The little voice of desire, silenced by perceptions of

workability

Take away them all…

I have conscientiously wrapped them for you,

In a chartered plane of freedom

With an added complimentary

Gift of gratitude

For enabling me to realize that

I have mine too!

My gifts are no less than yours

The illusion of understanding

The untruth of indispensability

The decision to choose

The choice to stay

The will to leave

The in transience of moments

I have bundled them too

And set them to sail

Far off unknown realms.

They are not needed-

Your gifts or mine

For the journey shall continue still

Unscathed by what we have to offer

Life, O Wonderful life

Let us hum to its music alone!

Perception

You say,

"We are two vessels, moving in tangential directions"

I think for a while

"We are rather two rivers, heading towards ocean".

How could it be otherwise?

I see the moon and the stars

Which illumine fields of your lunar imagination

And my terrains of creativity.

I bask in the glory of the same mellowed sun rays

That keep you warm

Amidst ice-cold glances

Furtive and indifferent.

I tread on the same earth

That directs you

To the destinations

Difficult, yet desired.

Your footsteps I hear,

Every night on the thoroughfare of my heart

Stealing my sleep ….asking me to be your companion

In the journey as dubious as our existence.

The waking life may be too dreary

Let me live with you in your dreams

As silently as the night that nurtures them

To spare you the pain of responsibility

Separated and united

Yes we are!

In what you perceive

As a tangential course

And I…as a bend in the river.

The Confession of Artemis

I, the alter-ego
Chaperoned by Artemis, every night,
Wandered in the wilderness of woods and
Landscapes of agile mind
The body's call
The flesh's squeal
Armed with the quiver of conscience
Decimated.

The unbridled gaiety
The golden shaft
The reckless gaze
Sentinels of chastity;
Till one night
Unguarded
I looked at you
My hunting companion-Orion
Defenseless, breathless…clad in silence

The golden face and heart outshined the golden shaft

Besotted hunting dalliances

The roving eyes

Stilled

In one moment of thy gaze

An endearing –invigorating gaze that inspires

Outlandish reversal of roles

Accomplished in shrine of love

In your light, O Orion

From sweet November to somber February

The hunter becomes the hunted

In pervasiveness of your brightness

I the Artemis, refuse to hide

Mellowed by the realization(s)

That joys and clamor of surrender

Are melodious than trumpets of victory

When love hunts,

It is wiser to be a prey.

Entreaty

You fear that love that has not blossomed yet
Might be killed by the miles between us
That the baby steps of understanding
Would breathe their last for want of support
That I might enclose you like
An overcast sky and that
You may be drenched unawares.

You fear that symbiotic union with me
Does that remind you of the umbilical connection
That was so hard for you to bear
Smeared with amniotic fluid of love and protection
You sought freedom
It did come at last…
Do you love it now, when you have it?

My caution smitten love
I don't intend to steal your idle hours
Or to undo your moments of silent speculation
I just want to be
A smile that begins in your eyes
And dies on your lips
Or a tear that never found its way onto your face.

I would rather be the central frame of your specs
That you so dotingly adjust on your forehead
Lost in profound thoughts or readings
Or perhaps that half formed arc
Beneath your eyes
Else the tick tock watch
That embraces your heart while you sleep.

Let me stay awhile
To
Listen to the rustling of your heartbeats
See your half-shut morning eyes
Touch your smooth hands
Feel the warmth of our togetherness
And believe the immortality of transitory life.

For then, even if going is inevitable
I will carry your fragrance
And the depth of big beady eyes

Not to forget the silken softness of your heart

To far off lands and unknown destinations
In the hope that…
Someday, you would come, searching for your lost
treasure.

Labyrinth

Stop walking

And the roads disappear

Into labyrinth

Squashed by the pricking thorns of conscience

The breath is diluted

By unkempt promises to self

The surging waves of anger

Directed at self

Ripples of angst

Seeping through the soul

Pacified by a sudden splash of awareness…

It is in rowing

Untethered …from the shackles of guilt and self-reproach

That my boat shall reach the shore.

Restrain

Do not be deceived
By that fixed gaze and half-lit smile
It has more tales to tell
Than the old grandma who lives in the old house.

Do not search for some soothing thoughts
In the crevices of puffy eyelids
They have found a way
Out of myriad rivulets of tears and smiles.

Do not compare that frizzy hair
If you would, with some raven cloud
They are the rough edges of life
Smoothened by acceptance.

Attempt, if you must: an understanding (of)
The strength engraved in heart.
The face behind the mask
The veil fixated on being.

Defiance

Your freedom to choose
My decision to surrender
I defy.

Your moving on
My halting
I defy.

Your taking life for granted
My being over-cautious
I defy.

Your non-willingness to lead
My helplessness to follow
I defy.

Your overlooking what you see
My being blind
I defy.

The Color Of Monday Is Blue

The color of Monday is blue
So are your eyes
And the vast ocean
Or the endless skies

Associations mingle
Certain gloominess
Hovers above them all
Supplementing a tinge of mystery

Perfected hue- perhaps a sense of pride
The color of aloneness is blue
And so is the color of strength
For all it bears, forbears and lets go

The blue veins that throb with life
Constantly move, unaware of their solitude
Or may be assured of their will
To be…just be!

The color of labor pain is blue
Death too, wears its somber shade
Ah! I had never realized
The irony and beauty of it!

The Vision

Sitting in a library,
Startled by a sound of 'thud',
I looked across the glass pane,
A dropped bag...a sense of unease...and an anxiety,
A quick calculation...movement of feet....bag located
Sans eyes...

It made me wonder...
Wonder about the times when people
Overlook the helpless beggar cornered in the street,
When I escape looking into the eyes of people
I am not on speaking terms with
Or prefer not to....

It made me reflective
About myriad unanswered questions,
About countless inquisitive looks,
Given to me, by the ones who were less fortunate.....
Piercing my soul asking...
What did I do to deserve this?

It made me recall the oft-repeated moments,

When we were too busy making calls, sitting in our luxury
cars

While a blooming young girl caressing a crying child asked
for a coin or two!

When on Valentine's eve a kid tried to sell me

A bunch of Roses....

Manifestation of love....

Ah! That reminds me...

What a bliss love is, with all its consequential troubles...

Something which that kid could never philosophize about...

As his concerns were too small....

Three meals a day

 And just a shelter to sleep!

This vision has awakened my senses

Only to make me realize

How blurred my vision of and towards life is...

Bestowed with the finest of eyes!

Defense

Pointing fingers,
In the pale-lit corners of a room
Wearing the apparel of logic
Balancing the conversation with counter arguments
I refute what you propose
You flout what I say.

The slumbering angry man in me
Finds a eureka moment
Banging the door
Un-doing the realm of anemic yellow light
I enter my world of fluorescent brightness
The angry man dies- dazzled by awareness.

What was it actually all about?
Defense- I Guess;
Of the opinions held, experiences lived;
Of the hurt received and the pain inflicted;
Defense- from the demons inside
And the stark nakedness of the truth.

May be I have still a way to go
To know, to feel...to realize
That I don't need to defend myself or the other
That if I am happy with my truth
It has not to be stamped so by others
That I have to let them be...with their individual truth.

I defy thou defense...thou shall live no more
Because I know...I simply know
I am not at war!

Echoes of Silence

Words desired...unheard

Expression required....amiss

That empty feeling in stomach

Tears inside....persecuted

Rationality expected....imposed

Emotions breathing....emasculated

The core of being....unfulfilled and incomplete

The echoes of silence go farther than you imagine!

Eyes

The movement of eyes
Communicative
Of Acceptance
Consent
Satire
Seduction...

The Universe is created
And crumbles
The Archer wins
And the Prey looses
The Photographer rejoices
And the object is bereft of a part of itself...

With mere
Movement of eyes.

The dancer moves
And the feet travel involuntarily
The silent language of eyes
Partakes
Supersedes
Language.

With mere
Movement of eyes.

Survival

Oh! It is just a phase
I tell myself.
The pain,
Anxiety,
Helplessness,
And refusal.

Nights which don't seem to end,
Days that are too bright to see;
For tear filled eyes.
Memories that refuse to bid goodbye,
Arguments that start in mind;
But never reach lips.

Oh! It is just a phase
I tell myself.

Sobs lost in humdrum of life,
Frustrations hidden beneath veneer of normalcy,
Desires crying to be   fulfilled,
Unborn wishes craving for life;
Scarce laughs interspersed with
An occasional drop at the corner of an eye.

Oh! It is just a phase
I tell myself!

In this struggle between love and survival
I choose survival!

Spaced Spaces

The spaces between you and me
Have begun to encroach upon
My mind's landscape
Like an uninvited serpentine trespasser
Intruding into the Garden of Eden.

Brutally undoing the innocence
Of child-like love
Ravishing the celestial beauty
Of feeling, dangling from the branches of trust.
Questioning the transience of intimacy.

Those spaces suffocate
With the space they occupy
Uproot or nurture?
One entails absence in absence
Another presence in absence.

What to choose?
The Amnesia or the nostalgia?

The Other

Being the other
I am blamed
For the crimes
I did not commit
I am troubled
By the moments
I did not live
I am accused
By voice of my conscience.

Being the other
I spend sleepless nights
Wanting to be 'The One'
I maintain the safe distance
Even from my true feelings
I am caged
In the bygone time
I am mocked at
By new memories you create.

Being the other
I want to sever all the ties
The ones that entwine my body and soul
I need to undo automatic playback –
Your smile, your eyes…you
I must move on
To the realm of otherness
I should internalize
That I am…the other.

The Desert Stars

You promised to spend a night in lap of the desert stars
Among the unknown, strange, unkempt footprints on sand,
Knowing perhaps that the imprints of our love too
Would be subsumed in that transient moment in space and
time.

Bodies love soiled …creases of desire
Hearts consumed, not by consummation
But discourse of 'before' and 'after'
The intellect wins the battle.

The glistening forms
Clad in sand
Both are beautiful
Only in unison

The desert stars would silently smile
Feigning indifference
Yet know
What it is to be 'the desert and the stars'!

Disconnect

The still child born
Seeks disconnect
From the umbilical cord
A mother's heart resists.

The autumnal withered leaves of friendship
Seek disconnect
From the branches that no longer nourish them
The tree disapproves.

The flickering flame of love
Seeks disconnect
From the windy ways and the ice –cold shoulders
The wick denies.

The caged bird of hope
Seeks disconnect
From the concrete steel bars of reality
The possessor abnegates.

The egoistic interiority of my being
Seeks disconnect
From your precarious presence
I accept.

The disconnect
Seeks to disconnect
From the embers of connect
And… surrenders.

Sneak In, My Love

Sneaking is your art, my beloved
Into the fortified castle of my being.
From the undulated cravings
Of your body,
A gush of warmth inundates;
To reach me.

Mesmerized by need
Smitten by desire
That begins in your eyes,
And reach me through the glances
I feel the shudder, untouched yet
Ravished …by will.

The cornucopia of your being and body
Alluring, Appeasing, Tempting
Defies my assertions of restraint
Just when the fire begins to die out
Kindled it is,
By some primeval instinct.

Benighted desires aglow with passion
Propel to unfathom you
Gently subsume the softness of your skin
The innocence of your face
The whisperings of your heart
The wild cravings of your body.

With the tips of my fingers
And the rosiness of my lips
I shall make you anew, my love
Re-writing the contours of your body
The boundaries of erotic
Blur…become one with the actuals

The whetted appetite
Unfulfilled, Unsatiated
Snubs the distance of miles
The aroma that you exude
Insinuates…
Me to be earth
Pregnant with your seed.

Sneak in, my love!

Wings

The clutched wings of freedom

Swayed by the voluntary winds of free will

Seek flight, fight or fright

Caught in the immanence of choices

The bird must learn acceptance.

Abandoned

Drooping branches,
Half-baked building
Light pierces the very soul of darkness
Through the window pane.

Reflection of light beams shivering
On the bosom of barren tree
Seem to watch, with agony,
The plight of men
Who come and go!

The place has been deserted?
Or the human race?
The question remains unanswered.

Oh yes! This time it is different,
The place has abandoned the man!

Me (a) lo(a)dy

Plants breathe,
I have been told!
Men too...I know.
There is a melody.

Of late a Mango tree in my garden
Has been panting;
I guess it needs oxygen pump...
And so does the old man,
Living next to the industry I work in.

For the avarice of few,
They will die!

The Glass House

The glass house

And your reflection

Both have shattered

I move past both…

For the twinge

And the blood stained heart

Is beyond repair

Some wounds heal…

Some are meant to be devoured.

The I-ness

In the vastness of I
A little voice rises and dies
Unaware of its object of search
The empty words or full hearts
Seem to drag, like a long summer day.

The destinations reached are perhaps obsolete
Till one replaces them with the newer pastures to explore
Well could I cry with Sisyphus
At the absurdity of in-box and out-of-box choices
Or like Icarus try to over-reach my waxen wings of desire
Seek may be Buddha's middle-path
Or the way of river.

The dew-drops of peace or solace
Would you touch me then
In your pristine glory?
Or I have to mediate...meditate
On the Now and here of this unease and restlessness?

May be...the answers I seek are nearer than I thought
May be...I am asking the wrong questions
May be...I must be cradled in the lap of silence
Till I am re-awakened and enlightened
Once again to the miracle of life

In the vastness of I
A little voice must be silenced...
To listen to what the vastness speaks of.

Monologue

The words have taken a long vacation

Unasked, unapproved,

Unsanctioned.

Either there is too much to say...

Or nothing.

JOURNEY

That lingering memory while
Listening to a song
Traveling by the train and the subconscious.

Reminds me of that unexplainable feeling
When one has outgrown the teens
But insists like a kid to stay back.....
To stay back in that time and space.

The feel of snow-clad mountains
That rush of adrenaline
Coupled with the melody of emotion
Unspoken and unheard.....

Love that has not flowered yet
But is in the embryonic form
Which may be delivered
Lest aborted by contraceptives of logic and reality.

The Innocent Step

The Step Forward
In Life
And Thought
Does not obliterate
The Road Taken
The errors of desires
Or mistakes of conscience.

The Step Backward
In Life
And Thought
Does not Re-create
The magic of dreamy nights
The Drunkenness of successful days
Or the taste of crazy days.

The Step, nonetheless
Completes the journey.

Cognition

I know the answers to questions
You do not ask…
Diluting them with a peculiar sense of
Irrelevance and Vagueness

I understand the silences
You defer or maintain
Consciously cultivated
Like moves of chess.

I sense the willing suspension
Of belief and disbelief
Rambling like spindle
From the alleys of your heart.

I perceive the untold truths
Slithering and simmering
Beneath the surface
Clamoring to be heard.

I can read your eyes
And their journeys
From sadness to laughter
And the occasional halts.

I know the answers to the questions
You do not ask
Diluting them with a peculiar sense of
Irrelevance and vagueness.

The Separated One

The tooth-brush in the stand
Kajal- liner pencils carelessly sleeping on the small glass
shelf
The shirt once cherished, hanging despondently behind the
bathroom door.

The two coffee mugs, one with lipstick stains
And few left-overs
The Creased sofa-covers,
defending
the sacredness of love that was shared.

The aesthetic handwriting on the menu list
Decorating the kitchen,
To-Do list
magnetized on the Refrigerator.

The separated one
Still occupies this home!

Of Yellow Book Pages and Swiveling Chairs

He met her with his fragrant yellow book pages dreams
And long conversations about the
Giant fog of love
Encompassing everything
Connecting everything to everything.

Little slow with mobile phones
And agile with his words
He served his words in right measures
And right portions
To tempt the fragile beloved.

They would discuss for hours
Things beyond the mind and body
To come back to its primal instincts
And accept with fortitude
That they were enthralled with prism of togetherness.

Till one fine day
The autumnal hue takes over
the scarlet passions
And he leaves his swiveling chair and yellow pages of a
read book
For her to make sense...for eternity.

Epiphyte

It is amazing
How in the matrix of life
You meet a co-traveller
Love his dimpled smile
Or his silver tongue
And then you part your ways.

You continue marching straight
And left and right
Though often at some turning points
You look hazily
At the faces
Searching for that one face
That chose oblivion
For you did not meet his sensual appetites.

Your mocking self
Sarcasm-clad
Asks
How could you be a traveller?
If your quest begins and ends
At one unnamable face?

You have perhaps just
One thing to murmur:
It has grown to live like an epiphyte on me...
I thrive on its memories.

Woman

You cannot look through her soul

Or understand

The pride she takes

In having stood through it all

Of suffering, winning and losing

Or standing tall

Only the companions in struggle know

What it is to be a woman

And not give up.

The Flying Carpet

I want to make a flying carpet of words

Embellish it with a simile here

And a metaphor there

To travel

Far beyond my judgments

And your opinions

With wings of faith and courage

I shall seek

My ever-changing destinations

Happy to realize that

All going in itself

is Arriving.

The Game Of Numbers

Love, no matter, when it arrives
Settles its roots
In the space of your being.

At eighteen
with love letters and roses in your hands
you would think- it's different
At twenty eight.
It isn't so...

At twenty eight
the love letters might refuse to be written in golden letters
But you will find some words
Hanging on the lips
Or certain tears hiding
As you exchange a hug or embrace
with the man you love
or woman you adore.
Twenty-eight, then, is an age of subtlety.

Don't let the numbers be-fool you

The age-ness of age

Cannot...does not

spare you

Of crazy thoughts and panic attacks

The fear of loss or heartache of separation;

It still...

Brings a blush on your face

Or that naughty smile..

With its shrewd ways...

It always...

Makes your heart palpitate...

And your eyes sparkle.

Love, no matter when it arrives,

Settles its roots

In the space of your being.

All About Love

Sometimes, Love hurts
Like an earthen lamp smashed on an angry night
The lamp that cried and embraced
The memories of the glass you just broke.

Sometimes, Love surprises
Like a sudden rain shower
On the night you decided to leave for home early
To discover your kids cuddled up in a blanket.

Sometimes, Love speaks
Like a nightingale in the woods
When the lovers sit silently
Reading the irresistible depth of eyes.

Sometimes, Love smiles
Like that naughty kid in the street corner
When she steals some glances
In the meditation hall to send you a flying kiss.

Sometimes, Love strikes

Like a shooting arrow

In moments when long lost memories

Nudge you to the brim of insanity.

Sometimes, Love grows

Like an epiphyte

On the roots of your soul

To teach you the lessons of surrender and freedom.

Sometimes, Love defies

Any expression

It is in its muteness

And silent ways

That it becomes the greatest.

Sometimes, Love completes

Unlike anything

The form and the being

Of who you are or could be!

I Want To Love You...

I want to love you
Like an eclipsed night
Spread out....
Endlessly...
Stretching till eternity...

Or like a dew-drop on a flower
Attached for micro-moments
Free forever
To seep in...

Perhaps like that last tear
Which grows in throat
And is uprooted
Mingled with heart
As a memory...

I want to love you
Like dim-yellow light lamps
On ice-cold foggy night streets
Inspiring
The tired steps that I don't wish to tread...

I want to love you...
Like I have not loved anyone else.

On Indian Love Day

On Indian Love Day
Let me explain
What counts as love
And what does not!

When a woman equates a man
To the Moon
She ascribes to him only its beauty
And not its flaw...
That is love.

When a woman lets go
Of all her happiness
To make her man happy
And her soul is torn apart
For betraying herself
That is not love.

When she tinkles her bangles
Or her anklets
What she revels in
Is more of her happiness
At the music he brings
Than the pricey silver or gold
That is love.

When 'Nakshatra diamonds'
or 'Raymond suits'
Assume greater significance
Than a stolen kiss
Or a passionate embrace
That is not love

When he works to his best abilities
To let her have her way
And is scolded for turning up late
He is living love
More in Action
Than in words.
That is love

When the language of silence
Interspersed with monosyllables
Begins to gnaw
Than to create the
Ripples of bliss
That is not love

When he knows the difference
Between the smile she wears
And the smile she lives
That is love
When she understands
The words unsaid
And silent silences
That is love.

When they understand
That metaphors of moon
Or Mehandi
Are a soul's calling
To unite with their individual yet unified light
And not mere rituals
That is love...

Love, then is action
Supplemented by words.

The Drip

The life flows through the drip
Unto the life withering with pain
Syringe,Scissors...simmering tension
And my friend on a hospital bed.
A clandestine reflection
The pricking ending of relationships,
The jarring betrayals and heart breaks
The entrenched agony fixated in soul.
Heal...sans the external stimulus
The inner work...the awakened being
The dialogues with self , the phoenix form
Ah! What a miracle man is!

The Finality

In the end

You will just remember

The people you loved

And the people who loved you

Rest...remains a long held grudge

Not worth the effort.

Purgation

You now wash the dirt and grime
Off his clothes
And may be the musk of his desires
Acted out in moments of temptation and profound love.

It is a story from another night though
I too, washed the outer agencies of defilement
Off his clothes
With a reverence of a worshiper driving away mere dust
from the holy feet.

You carry the perfume of consummation
Perhaps in the margins of your body
I emanate the fragrance of lived reality with him
In my words and deeds.

You have sneaked in his body and heart
Like a column of breath
I pervade his life
Like a half forgotten memory that refuses to budge.

Purged, shall we be
You, of what remains of smithereens of your being
I, of what could have been
And fortunately, is not.

And They Lived Happily Ever-After...

Yes, that was the dream!
To live happily ever-after,
As I left my home
To adorn some other world;
Some alien hearts!

The seven rounds with seven vows
Around the sacred fire,
Millions of hopes weaved in;
Thousands of desires blushing;
Mingling with the bridal glow on my face!

The scarlet 'kumkum' sealed my fate
Tied to the anklets of subversion
Enclosed in the bangles of restrictions
I still managed to smile and move
Into the house, they call my own!

My idolized husband
Made love to me every night,
Reaching happily to the body I wear
Ignoring, ridiculing...defiling,
An abyss of my lovelorn heart.

A year and thirty have passed,
With myriad compromises and sacrifices.
A daughter and a son,
Are my rewards,
For the lost happiness and gained respect.

Sometimes though, I hear
The tinkling sounds of promising hopes
As I see my daughter defying
The norms and restraints
To choose the man she loves.

In the dimmed corridors of age,
Faltering, with withered senses and a hazy vision
Wearing the masks of a happy woman
And an adorable wife;
I still await my happily ever-after moments.

Ripple Of Thought

The droplet that became the ocean

And never faced

Identity crisis

We humans...

Have a knack of complicating things.

The Language Cloud

The language cloud
Hovering above my train of thoughts
Does not settle
Either at turquoise lonely days
Or empurpled crazy nights.

The bellowing winds of exasperation
Or howling screams of mind
Do not...
Can not...
Undo its existence.

My Language cloud smiles at
Thoughts that refused to be penned
Words that deny identity
Sentences that are aborted in making
Discourses that are dissected by senses.

It is only when I realize
That I am the stabile sky
I let go of the language cloud
Or its stubbornness to shower me with bliss
For I am its creator and destroyer
"Aham Brahmsami"

Invictus (The Sequel)

You call me a woman
Gendered,
Sometimes jeered,
Sometimes jarred.

You have a clear idea of
How I should Look or Dress;
And even the way i am supposed to make love
Or behave in the crowd.

Nonetheless-
I make my own constructions
Of what i am
Or what you could
make out of me.

Your judgments pin me down
with their weight
And then suddenly
I feel lighter
As you light that cigarette to attend to your anxiety calls.

A mere spark of fire

Can undo your masks of strength

May be then

Its you and not me

Who needs to be protected-

Protected, not in the sense you protect me

But from your own uneasy thoughts

That drive you to make decisions

that you won't

If you knew more about being and less about gender.

No matter how enticing the temptation

No matter how deep the call of power

You and me...my man

Are the masters of our fate

And the captain of our souls.

epilogue

Sakshi Chanana

about the *A*uthor

Sakshi Chanana is an Indian poet writing in English. Poetry for her is a way of being that defines and shapes human life. Her academic credibility can be judged from her being a gold-medalist in English literature as well as her recent submission of PhD. Theses at Centre of English studies, J.N.U, New Delhi, India. Her poems have been published in national and international journals and anthologies like 'Muse India', 'Kritya', 'Reading Hour', 'A Few Lines Magazine', 'Tajmahal Review' and 'Inner Child Press Magazine'. A traveller at heart and academician by choice, she has been continually engaged in reading, research, learning and teaching. In her words, "All going in itself...is arriving". A die-hard optimist, a cheerful teacher and a lover of words, she stands apart with her tiny hope to make world a better place to love and live.

Acknowledgements

I would like to express my heartfelt gratitude to all the people who helped me in the successful completion of this most cherished project of my life. I would like to thank Inner Child Press- William S. Peters and Janet Caldwell for providing me with such opportunity and carrying on commendable task of spreading poetry with the vision of beautiful world order of love, happiness and peace. My thanks are due to my dear Professor Saugata Bhaduri, who took time out of his busy schedule to be a part of it and encouraging me in my literary pursuits.

I am also indebted to my dear friend Birat Krishna Thapa for continuously supporting me in the entire process of writing, editing and completing the work. Many thanks are also due to my wonderful friends who were always there to listen and offer their kind suggestions: Mahwash, Shelley, Ankita, Arundhati, Ritwick, Kanika, Meha, Didier. Kanchan Bhattacharya, Sumedha and Radhika. I would be more than happy to thank all my fans of Facebook poetry page for their constant encouragement. My special thanks are due to Jen Walls for her unconditional love, concern and for being a medium to materialize this project.

I am thankful to Prof. Vinod Verma for not only guiding me but also for his timely help in selection of book cover design. I am also grateful to Harish Agawane for his contribution to author pictures as well as to Karandeep who facilitated the photo-shoot.

This work would not have been possible without endless love and support of my family- my Mom, my Papa and my adorable sister Shikha. I have been divinely blessed to have huge share of blessings and affection from my extended family- my cousins, relatives and all lovely little kiddos. Finally, I acknowledge and thank that powerful spirit which makes me write...makes me create...makes me live.

Inner Child Press

Inner Child Press is a Publishing Company Founded and Operated by Writers. Our personal publishing experiences provides us an intimate understanding of the sometimes daunting challenges Writers, New and Seasoned may face in the Business of Publishing and Marketing their Creative "Written Work".

For more Information

Inner Child Press

www.innerchildpress.com

intouch@innerchildpress.com

www.ingramcontent.com/pod-product-compliance
Lightning Source LLC
Chambersburg PA
CBHW060807110426
42739CB00032BA/3125